First published by Publishing Genius Press
www.publishinggenius.com

ISBN 978-1-945028-26-7

Cover drawings by Robyn O'Neil
www.robynoneil.com

Book design by Adam Robinson

$50,000 ANDREW WEATHERHEAD

PUBLISHING
GENIUS PRESS

"Friends cost money."

—*James Baldwin*

The boxer Zab Judah has been mugged by the rapper
Fabolous twice

The sun rising on W. 27th Street, the sodium lights hum
on 10th Ave

The form of life or the sound or the color of life

The soul spasms in the space left for it by the flesh

Facts are innocent, like flies in a room, not even looking for a way out

I walk around naked, turning lights off

A. thinks we have bed bugs

The bites on his arms are horrible, but they aren't bed bugs…

The cat sleeps in my chair

What should I do?

It flies around the room, just out of reach—

Words only get in the way

Sirens doppler in the distance

Time smothers us, as if it's not enough

When B. and I went to Stonehenge, there was no
mystery left to solve

Built by agrarian tribes around 3000 BC—it's a burial
ground

And 5 quid later, we got in another fight when I paid
with my credit card instead of the local currency...

Not the first, not the last, but representative of
everything that had happened and would

We both thought money was love, in its own way

Real, austral, frank

Sovereign, scarce, and fungible

The world appears when you least expect it

Class action lawsuit against my old gym: $166.11

But the poem quivers, vanishing on approach

Boredom creates an impatience with one's life, and a violence to improve it

Loneliness creates a detestation for losing

My boss closes his door and takes a call

I'm at my desk listening to Ravel

Unhappy that I can't know anything other than myself

C. comes to fix the copier

His walk is spooky, like there's a gun pressed against his head

He cuts the wrong wire

The room fills with smoke

D. runs to the door

As I watch through a wall

My forehead pressed against the glass

Rising on a word and falling on a syllable

It's 73 degrees, September 4th

There's an ad for porn on dictionary.com

They found water on Mars

I want to talk to E., but I have nothing to say

Freckles like ellipses…

Another depressing weekend

Time stands still; we move through it

The blue, shiny buildings at the end of summer

Ships queue to enter the kill

Can't tell if it's foggy or if I'm just tired

More waves than birds, more birds than boats

Words present us with little pictures of things

So how is it possible to mean anything you say?

I feel like a circle: perfect in theory and impossible in reality

The days get shorter and shorter

While the names of the months get longer

The cat looks out the window

The universe vibrates at B♭

Time disappears into the seams of being

I glide like Gumby through the office

And pretty soon this too will be a memory

Mike Tyson: "I'm always quoting my heroes, it's never me talking"

Ted Berrigan: "I like credit cards"

Something crawls across my floor

My door makes a sad noise

It's what no one knows about you that allows you to know yourself

Allen Iverson stepping over Tyrone Lue

But this isn't a poem with an answer

It's about the fractal nature of wealth

The space between voids

Nightmares of typos

Grey light on greyer stones

More pigeon than dove

But some dove

The courtyard is silent

The sound of your own blood circulating

The night is cold and our passion for living is not well understood

My mind is tiny—so much smaller than my head

I don't care

I'm tired of comparisons

Error conquers wisdom

And faith conquers error

Right?

I get off the train and walk in the wrong direction

More symptom than cause

But the thing about writers is they all want to be someone else

It's the spring of 1995 and I'm carving my name into wet concrete—a construction worker grabs me by the shirt and makes me confess to my mom

It's the summer of 2005 and I'm spray painting my name on a billboard—a police officer grabs me by the shirt and makes me confess to my dad

But they don't know my real name: Kermit Rainman…

Sheila Dikshit…

Otis Overcash…

Ronuald Rat…

Co-Eric Riley...

Tedric Spider...

Jamal Criteria...

Bufus Dewberry...

Gates Peed...

Faux Zeke…

George Foreman on losing: "It's like being in a deep dark nothing, like out at sea, with nothing over your head or under your feet, just nothing, nothing but nothing. A horrible smell came with it, a smell I haven't forgotten, a smell of sorrow. You multiply every sad thought you ever had it wouldn't come close to this and then I looked around and I was dead. That was it. I thought of everything I worked for, I hadn't said good-bye to my mother, my children, all the money I hid in safe-deposit boxes, you know how paper burns when you touch it, it just crumbles. That was my life. I looked back and I saw it crumble, like I'd fallen for a big joke"

Rodney Dangerfield, after being told a joke: "Hey kid, I'm not one for jokes"

A sandwich board gloms onto the sidewalk

Brooms cough against the concrete

No one likes missing the bus except me

It's Tuesday

Twice this week I've seen people ask for the display
pastries at Starbucks, even after being told they were
only for display

Writing poems like invoicing a prior self

Actual ad concept from my job: "The dollar signs all fly down converging towards the girl, and she absorbs them"

Fingers move across a sticky keyboard

One of the interns asked us to check out her mixtape

F. started using astronaut lingo

He responds to my email: "Roger that"

And starts counting down from 10...

9...

8...

7...

6...

5...

4...

3...

2...

1...

Oprah Winfrey: "When I look into the future, it's so bright it burns my eyes"

Manny Pacquiao twitching on the canvas after an overhand right from Juan Manuel Marquez

Expensive sunglasses in my closet

Dreams of total narcissism and self-involvement

Google searches for emotions, feelings, bars near me

Rivers that never reach the sea

Feelings of anxiety, joint pain, and muscle soreness

Sudden loss of consciousness, seizures, stroke

ICD-10[1] code Y34: "Unspecified event, undetermined intent"

---

[1] The International Classification of Diseases, Tenth Revision (ICD-10) is a system used by physicians and other healthcare providers to classify and code all diagnoses, symptoms, and procedures recorded in conjunction with hospital care in the United States.

Being a writer means separating your unique ideas and feelings from those understood by everyone else, and that is one of the hardest and most painful things a person can do

Sat outside the bank, listening to the wind

Was offended by something earlier, but now I can't remember what

Someone stole all the jump ropes from my boxing gym

And I found out I've been allergic to toothpaste this whole time

Alone in my room, it's like the world must appear—

Art and money… particle and wave… being and nothingness…

Watching football with roommates, I had no idea how to respond to the news that G.'s baby was born prematurely

I typed "Congrats!!!" before editing it to "Congrats!"

Then the day writhed in the wrong direction

The room went quiet, the lights were on

Everyone drifted slowly away from everyone else

But the dream still starts at the door

They call your name when your coffee's ready:

Larry Koldsweat...

Carl Crumpler...

Dean Windass...

Charles Fugger...

H. complains about his credit union and his son

I. dreams about the Hulk and punches his wife

This morning I listened to three coworkers try to remember who Jeff Goldblum is

"I don't remember any white people in Independence Day" they said

And I ate lunch with J.

People age differently, she said

And time is a jelly

It wooshes

Constant fear is the natural state of man—a path from the real to the abstract

Gavrilo Princip finishes his sandwich, steps outside, and assassinates the Archduke Franz Ferdinand

World War I begins

World War I ends

Trees rustle overhead

Haven't experienced much tragedy lately

Except the anniversary of my dad's death, which was
four years ago yesterday

But that's just an anniversary

There was a time, three years ago, when it seemed everything went wrong

Towed cars, missed flights, stolen bike

Psychologically unstable roommate

Bed bugs, stolen mail

St. Patrick's Day

Hurricane Sandy...

But ends meet ends

My mouth full of small words

Words like aoijfs, cewc, and sxx

The culmination of thousands of years of
consciousness

Extending the limits of fear, pain, and self-loathing

Ecce—

The Everglades

The Pan-American games

3:33am, July 4th

High on cocaine

"I wish people never stopped growing, like trees," I said

And I was thinking of a root system that's long and thin

But I keep waking up in someone else's idea of the world, and I have no idea why

My mind laid down like a palm frond...

The pained beating of wings…

Until we're back where we began

$4.50 for iced coffee

Tater tots, untouched, in the trash

B-roll of hell

Stock photos of people losing the will to live

Every few hours a man with one eye walks by my desk

He sees the real me, eating lunch alone

Maybe Andy Warhol was right, making money *is* art

Connected with a stunt woman on LinkedIn

K. showed me videos of his horse

L.'s husband's name is also L.

They named their son M.

And I spun in my chair, thinking someone else's
thoughts

It's incredible that anything gets done—

The intercom's paging someone named *Ned Spaghetti*

Asia Larry...

Is this all there is?

There must be... something else...

The streetlights flicker on Church

Distance sweeps through the city like a plague

I played basketball every day for years and years until one day I just stopped

Now I'm emailing someone named Michael Jordan

Dear Michael Jordan,

My name is Andrew Weatherhead

I feel like a Venn Diagram—

Every Friday I'm asked "what are you doing this weekend"

And every Monday I'm asked "what did you do this weekend"

Now it's Wednesday

Doors open

Doors close

The wind stops, but the clouds keep moving

Joy Williams: "The day beat down upon them with its intimations of night"

James Baldwin: "The trees were blue and brown, purple and black"

Kiss the glass

Everyone else's problems seem worse

O. comes to work feverish again

No one wants to be near her, they cancel her meetings

P. gets out of his car and tosses his keys in the air

I walk quickly past Café Mogador, trying to stay cool

Friends of friends haunt me

Lunch meat drives me insane

Cus D'Amato: "The hero and the coward feel the same thing"

Vi Khi Nao: "My soul is a cul-de-sac"

But there's no problem sleep can't solve

So I let time have its way with me

The night like a polished stone

The augmented 4th between the fridge and the microwave

While melody tenderizes your pathetic soul...

Before enlightenment, worry about not being enlightened

After enlightenment, worry about not being
enlightened

Within each poem lies another, smaller poem

But there is no poem without me

So what if it wasn't love—

Cats don't really have nine lives

Planet Fitness isn't really a planet

Words are spiders

They string us along

The future and the past compete for regrets

And purgatory is the best I can hope for

Dominions of beige and fluorescent light

Long, thin fingers appear from behind the partition

Colville died last night

In the year we lived together, he never did his dishes

He would leave pots of water on to boil until the
pot was charred black and the apartment was full of
smoke

He would invite people over then leave and not
answer calls or texts

He got fired from an unpaid internship

I guess I never realized how sick he was

Though I was alone in liking his poems

Now I just feel awful for his parents

And I try to see what he saw

So a curtain breathes

A computer sighs

The floor fan shakes its head no

My face hurts from frowning again

ICD-10 code V97.33: "Sucked into jet engine"

Mike Tyson: "All of my heroes were truly miserable bastards, and I emulated them my whole career"

Exchanged phone numbers with the bodega guy

Accidentally said the name of a pornstar while trying to think of a coworker's name

An incognito browser for the soul

Q. moved to LA and joined the alt right

Light emanating from R.'s door

How transparent are our desires—

The infinite monkey theorem says that given an
infinite number of monkeys at an infinite number
of typewriters over an infinite amount of time, the
monkeys would eventually produce a great work of
literature

But an infinite number of monkeys given an infinite amount of time would never be able to recognize their work as great

Even to a literate human, an infinite amount of time would render a great work of literature meaningless

So in 2003, researchers in England gave six macaques a computer and a keyboard for a month

They produced five pages, mostly of the letter *s*, before the lead male destroyed the keyboard with a rock and the other five urinated on the computer

The letters *b*, *v*, and *q* crept in

Iceberg Slim: "A pink butterfly lay there like a silent indictment"

A layer of dust on the Num Lock key

Fyodor Dostoevsky: "We don't even know where the living lives now, or what it is, or what it's called"

Seagulls go "ga!"

Ralph knocks on the door

But I'm at work

Clicking here, clicking there

Drawing things to scale

Things like wonder, my salary, a notion of the world
in which I am valued

A coworker I've never met or heard of emailed to say goodbye and give me her contact info in hopes that we'll stay in touch

They fired S.

They fired T.

And I just sat down

It doesn't matter—

Beauty's not for the asking

Money is a measure of humiliation

Currency = value = confidence = perception = narrative

So the amount of bullshit in the world is staggering

The deli was closed, then it was open

What good is an explanation

Guy Debord: "Truth is a moment of falsehood"

33 people killed by ambulances last year

Pro-life politicians that support the death penalty

A United States of One-Way Streets

Facts can't change us; beliefs are too resilient

Agreeing to disagree may be all there is

Even though scientists guess we're all just guessing

Because if knowledge, then ignorance and fear

So I mistake spilled coffee for a shadow

Watch light slow down

No answers only interpretations

Ideas fly like birds into windows

But still lives happen

Potted plants hanging from the sill; vases rest on the floor

A cough comes through the wall—

The long, slow descent into yourself from which you
may never recover

A prison of preferences

This strategic arrogance

I feel like a spy who's forgotten his mission

Elizabeth Bishop: "the sensation of falling off the round, turning world into cold, blue-black space"

Grad school: $61,160

ICD-10 code Y92.241: "Library as place of occurrence of the external harm"

But I'm still waiting for the diagnosis that will set me free

Dread blooms on a Sunday

Sweating in the shower, dry skin in the summertime

I spread out like a sphere

A surface separate from ideas

Ursula Le Guin: "Truth is a matter of imagination"

So I'll believe anything

But believe in nothing

Now that I'm single, I probably won't go to the beach at all this summer

I'll sit home and justify all my flaws with what I remember of Zen Buddhism

e.g. if I misspell a colleague's name in an email, it is the Bodhisattva way

e.g. If I forget to hold the door for an elderly woman, it is the Bodhisattva way e.g. If I break up with my girlfriend in the middle of the night, drunk, because I'm afraid she might leave me first, it is the Bodhisattva way

But no matter how depressing this book may get, just think about how much positive thinking it must have taken me to finish it

Because I'm nobody—another reason not to talk

The older I get, the more comfortable I am with myself, the less validation I need from others, the less connection to society I feel, the more time I spend alone in my room shadow boxing

Sometimes I forget I'm not a member of the band
Fugazi

Tried to find out what time it is by looking at a
newspaper

So what if the earth is flat

Thelonious Monk gets up and takes a lap around the
piano

There are things in life besides the truth

But I *am* all alone in this conference room

Watching a cockroach escape into the ceiling

While outside a pigeon gets an idea

Snow melts slowly, like a gift

The same, grey wind—

Men without faces:

Suits with pinstripes, ties abstract with meaning

A music without sound

Michael Jordan crossing over Larry Bird

Allen Iverson crossing over Michael Jordan

Light from the computer screen while the city turns to dust

Hours pass...

Lie after lie delays the truth

Can't tell the difference between wisdom gained with age and an increasingly sophisticated construct of narcissism and self-justification

But I'm not unique, I can't be

This morning I listened to coworkers argue over the Spanish translation of *bok choy*

After fifteen minutes, they settled on *bok choy*

Words and feelings must be entirely separate then

i.e. I'm all glazed, like a donut

50,000 versions of the same poem

Numbers sweating words

The Ancient Greeks were terrified of the number zero

"How can nothing be something" they demanded

But the universe is dominated by dark energy,
something less than nothing

I feel like a standardized test

Left my credit card at KGB bar

And the tab stayed open for 84 hours

So I can't afford the truth

While in a dream, I chartered a jet to follow the sunset around

And woke covered in sweat

Unable to differentiate between what I said and what I wanted to say

Another book falls off the shelf through no force but its own

After the Bible, Gutenberg wanted to publish a treatise on laxatives

How many passing moods are being lived out elsewhere…

But I'm having obvious feelings again

I wonder what everyone's really thinking

And how nothing ever happens the way it actually happens

A.:   I'm sorry to do this over email. My notion was to hope for everyone to be around tonight so that I could talk to everyone at once, but considering that ████████'s living situation is imminently affected I think time is probably more important to you than the personal touch.

I've decided I'm not going to move out. I've also decided that I'm going to move my friends ████ and ██████ in. And this means that Andrew and ▌████████, you guys will have to move out. You can have until December 1st and ████████ is welcome to stay with us during that time (I'm assuming ██████ will be on board with this), but that's probably about as long as ████ and ████████

can push it at their current residence. You're welcome to move out beforehand, of course, but I figured two months was a minimal length of time to give you to find another situation. Andrew, ██████, perhaps you and ██████ can split half of the rent during the time that she's here, $400 each, with ████ and I paying $600 each? Between that and your deposits that would give you ~$900 to put towards a deposit on your next place.

I'm really sorry to do this. It's nothing personal at all. You've both been really good roommates, but want a different living situation. I'm especially sorry to be doing this to you after announcing that I was going to be the one moving out (and ██████, you can ████████ making plans based on that assumption), but it finally occurred to me that moving for me during the next couple of months is going to present a significant hardship, because of my knee surgery and that that's just not good for me. So, ultimately, I'm making a selfish decision and I'm very sorry that it fucks you guys over.

I'm going to talk to the landlord tomorrow and if you like I can inquire about other apartments that he might have available in our building or other buildings in the area? Should I ask him about 2BR or 3BRs?

If you're around tonight, we can talk more about this stuff, but I'll be sort of scarce in the evenings between Thursday and Sunday.

Theodore Roethke: "The world invades me again"

I'm all pink, like impatiens

A real touch-me-not

And no lie in the world can help

Someone knocks on the door

I don't get it—

I go out and make a mess

The floor around my wastebasket is warping because
I've vomited into it so many times

I go to work to distract from my life

Where my email signature just scratches the surface

Our names are what happens when you combine
secrets with facts

So you can call me *Sultan McDoom*

Shattice Bacon-Blood

Dick Posthumus

Harrison Treegoob

Jetsy Extrano

Joe Loser Jr.

Jimbob Ghostkeeper

Ham Biggar

Bea Swarm

Carlton Crunk

Lolita Respectnothing

I need better words for my anxieties—big, horrible
words

Last night I dreamed I was being mauled by a bear, a mountain lion, and a wolf simultaneously

Ominous laughter from the executive boardroom

Found someone's vampire screenplay on the printer

Now I'm watching the monkey paw sweat on the Mailchimp send screen

Sometimes I feel cut out, like a paper doll from a book, the perforated lines still stuck to my toes and under my arms—and other times I feel like I'm the one who's cutting the world to fit the shape I've given it

Just want to smoke weed and disappear

But in 24 to 48 hours I know I'll feel completely different

So I buy low and sell high on my sorrow

Because money is a kind of poetry

And the national debt is staggering

It's -5 degrees, February 4th

Everything can be reduced…

Quarks, leptons, bosons

U. chews her gum like a cow chews cud

Two of the guys from finance got stuck in the elevator
for an hour

They've been talking about it for weeks

I'm trapped in something less than history—

Can't think of anything besides food or sleep to look
forward to

Unsure of what anyone looks like

Joy Williams: "Amazing grace. The ways of fate. It's a blessing we can't comprehend them"

I may never know what "ontological" means

The world is always just beneath the surface anyways

V. told me that "the Grand Tetons" means "the Big Tits" in French

And that's all she could think about

They're playing "Footloose" in the post office again

I just want to have fun and party—

And with the cone on the cat's head, I can throw treats to her like I'm playing basketball

But now that I'm 31, my "divorced" status on Facebook isn't funny anymore

With money I become a different person, understand
a different passage of time

It's Friday—

Wealth is a virus, tearing the human race apart

The more we have, the more we want

Bands, bones, bread, bricks, bullets…

Cake, cheese, dough, roll, shrapnel, tender…

The Greeks went to war for love

Invented money to pay their soldiers

And invented literature to remember them

But history happens to each of us equally

So I'm writing this on my work phone

Spare room in back of my head—

Thinking about how cool it would be if there were
undiscovered office supplies the way there are
undiscovered bug species

Susan Howe: "There are names under things and
names inside names…"

Novice Nelson…

Squeegee Santillian...

Gooley Orr...

Proxy Rodriguez...

Muffin Lord...

Odd Striggles...

Bob Cum…

I think, therefore I am

Told someone I'm 34

Motifs > themes

They forgave all my student loans when my dad died

And mom said she's never going back to the house
again, ever, after an incident in which the woman
facilitating the estate sale fell and broke her ankle,
then returned to yell at our neighbor who thought she
was pricing things unfairly

Money changes people just like art, religion, or a
significant other

What am I missing?

The sound of a few leaves?

The void that makes real that which is not?

But didn't I say that already?

It wasn't supposed to rain today, not like this…

Some things that have been used as money: salt,
slaves, cocoa, cacao, capes, feathers, teeth, large and
hard-to-move stones, knives, scalps, skulls

They found water on Mars again

But it won't help us

Language is too lazy

The lifespan of a fact is as short as it's ever been

Each present's more prescient than the last

The door swung open and the taxi driver said "come with me if you want to live" after four gunshots across the street

Deep, crude deposits of rage in each person's being

The pipes clang with abandon

The entire office is buzzing with Amber Alerts

[Insert emotionally potent oversimplification]

Joy Williams: "One of the great secrets of life is learning to live without being happy"

So I go home and go to sleep

Two black holes—me and not me—competing for my
soul

The world arises in some way or other—

Sandstone, siltstone, shale, coal, sandstone, siltstone,
shale, coal

Talking to some coworkers I feel I can see their entire
lives

W. said "step into my office" and led the auditors into the kitchen

One of the graphic designers admitted he's colorblind

And you'll never believe what happened next...

They caught X. masturbating in his cubicle

Y. stole a stack of laptops

The Warriors blew a 3-1 lead in the finals

Donald Trump became the 45th president of the
United States

Facts are lonely things

They wander the world, like radio signals, dying for a
receiver

400 billion birds—

1.1 million cops—

Charles Darwin married his first cousin, Emma

We hold these truths

But the people who say they'd die for their art never do

The end is in the beginning

The cat gets stuck under the couch

Left my credit card at KGB bar again

And my debit card at the sports bar across the street

And when I went to retrieve it they said the tab was $0
because I didn't order anything (?)

I signed the check anyways

And left feeling upset with myself for being upset with myself being upset with myself

Some more words for nothing: oh, love, diddly, wind, scratch, ought, duck, doughnut

William Carlos Williams: "Time does not move. Only ignorance and stupidity move"

Styles make fights

It's raining; it's snowing

The brain tricks the heart into caring

And there's no one to complain about the weather to
when you're unemployed

Can't see Manhattan, New Jersey, or Staten Island
through the fog

My knees, shaking

Sha na na na knees, knees

The Uzbeks just sit there smiling

The bus driver just laughs

The poem sneaks up on you

John Ashbery: "Once you've lived in France, you don't want to live anywhere else, including France"

The body is fine, but the soul takes a turn for the worse

ICD-10 code X52: "Prolonged stay in weightless environment"

And one of the trainers at my boxing gym got struck by lightning

Writing poetry is easy—

I write *I'm wearing a wire*

And slide the notebook across the table, before they walk me out of the building

I really hate reality, I hate what it's done to me

Birds chirping in my right ear, the BQE in my left ear

Two helicopters fly into the same cloud

Z. quit seeming, but...

Joy Williams: "There aren't the words for half of what goes on in this life"

It feels like I'm floating but I know I'm not

So I write the same sentences over and over again

Truly believing that's what life is, which it is

It's a quarter past nine—the paper is cold, the pen is frozen

The last words spoken on the moon were "forget the camera"

I wish I had something to say

Leanna   ●●●

YOU MATCHED WITH LEANNA ON 3/19/16

Hey

 Hey how are you?

Good, how are you doing?

 Good thanks and you?

Mar 19, 2016, 7:18 PM

Good and you?

 Good thanks

Good

Sent

GIF   Message   Send

Acknowledgements

Sections of this book have appeared in different forms in the publications *NY Tyrant* and *Logue* [yellow]. Thank you Jordan and David.

The author would like to thank the following people, whose support and encouragement made this book possible: David Fishkind, Molly Brodak, Jordan Castro, Blake Butler, Tao Lin, Zachary German, Adam Robinson, Shane Jones, Jordan Daley, Ann Weatherhead, and Griffin, Bubba, and Celeste Fraser.

The lists of names in this book were procured from nameoftheyear.com.

Andrew Weatherhead is the author of the poetry collections *Cats and Dogs* (Scrambler Books, 2014) and *Todd* (Monster House Press, 2018). He lives in New York City and used to work in health insurance.

CPSIA information can be obtained
at www.ICGtesting.com
Printed in the USA
FSHW010201051219